Growing Herbs

A Beginner's Guide to Herb Gardening at Home

Table of Contents

Introduction

Do you like gardening? Do you like the idea of growing herbs at home? Do you want to start an herb garden at home, but don't know where to start? If yes, "Growing Herbs: A Beginner's Guide to Herb Gardening at Home" is the perfect book for you.

You don't need a green thumb to start gardening. If you have never tried your hand at gardening, it can seem intimidating. However, as with anything else in life, a little planning and preparation are needed. The first step to start gardening is to learn more about it. Irrespective of whether it is the balcony, terrace, or even the windowsill, you can create your little corner of paradise with an herb garden. Tending the herbs, watching them grow, and finally harvesting them, there is a lot to look forward to.

Herbs are easy to grow and maintain. They also offer versatility and are the perfect fit for beginners. Herbs provide a variety of medicinal properties and can be used in cooking. When used in cooking, they can instantly elevate the flavor profile of any dish. If using fresh herbs appeals to you, start following the tips and steps given in this book.

In this book, you will learn about the benefits of growing herbs at home, steps to start an herb garden, different methods of growing herbs, and gardening ideas for small spaces. You will learn about the ten best herbs suited for a beginner's herb garden and some tips to get you started. Once you are armed with all this information, herb gardening will not seem intimidating. If you are excited and eager to learn more about all this, let's get started immediately.

Chapter One:

Introduction to Herbs

I n the culinary world, the word herb is used to describe the leafy green part of a plant used to season or flavor a recipe, but it isn't used as the main ingredient. This definition isn't entirely right, because spinach is a green part of the plant, but it is not an herb and is a vegetable. Likewise, lettuce is also not an herb, but it is the green part of a plant. So, what is an herb? All plants that have aromatic and fragrant properties are known as herbs. Herbs are not only used to flavor foods but are also commonly used in natural medicines such as Ayurveda and even the cosmetic industry. Some common examples of herbs are rosemary, basil, parsley, dill, and thyme.

History of Herbs

Herbs are commonly used in cooking and help complement and enhance the flavor profile of different ingredients used. For instance, adding fresh basil to pasta or rosemary to potatoes changes the flavor profile of the entire dish. Fresh herbs have a stronger aroma than dried ones. The vitamin content and intensity of fresh herbs is quite stronger than the dried variants. Humans have been using herbs for over millennia now. It's not just culinary uses, but herbs even have medicinal applications. We have all been using herbs since ages to flavor and preserve food.

Herbs are commonly used in holistic healing systems such as Ayurveda, which dates backs to more than 5000 years. It relies on herbs and spices for their medicinal properties to heal the body and mind. Somewhere between 300 BC-200 A.D., a book about different medicinal plants was written in China, which was based on the knowledge passed on by Emperor Shen Nong. The book included information about more than 300 plants their medicinal uses and techniques for seed preservation. These plants were also classified based on their strength and toxicity.

The Ebbers Papyrus dates back to circa 1550 BC and is an Egyptian medical paper, including information about various herbs. It included more than 500 plant-based remedies for common medicinal problems. During the first century B.C. and 2nd century A.D., Hippocrates and Galen, famous Greek thinkers and doctors, came up with different herbal remedies as a form of treatment. Hippocrates, the father of modern science, believed in the healing properties of herbs. Colonists and settlers discovered several native herbs and plants used for medicinal purposes by the indigenous tribes. For instance, Echinacea is an herb native to North America and is commonly used to treat infections. It is still used for this purpose these days.

The healing power of herbs indeed withstood the test of time and unsurprisingly, the pharmaceutical drugs. We used these days, based on botanical ingredients are used to treat the same conditions which were identified by the business ages ago. So, it's not just your cooking that improves with herbs; you can also improve your health.

Benefits of Growing Herbs at Home

Fresh Herbs

Perhaps the most significant benefit of growing herbs at home is that fresh herbs will always be available at your fingertips. You don't have to go to the grocery store or wait for fresh produce at the farmer's market. Now, you can grow herbs at home. You merely need to pluck a few leaves from the potted plants as required. Irrespective of whether you are growing them indoors or outdoors, you will always have the ingredients you need. Organically grown herbs taste better than once grown using chemicals and harsh fertilizers. They are also more nutritious than regular ones available on the markets. Whenever any harmful inorganic chemicals and fertilizers are used, the nutrients are absorbed by the plant, but they also absorb all the other harmful chemicals present. These chemicals slowly make their way into the food chain. Prevent all this by growing your own producer home.

Seasonal Adaptation

You no longer have to wait for the right weather to grow the herbs you want. You can stimulate natural light using artificial grow lights and maintain your indoor garden irrespective of the season. Most herbs are quite forgiving and can survive in harsh conditions. All you need to do is water and fertilize them with organic fertilizers, take care of their soil requirement, and provide sufficient light. Once these four things are taken care of, you can pretty much grow any herb you want.

Creative Space Utilization

You don't need to worry about space requirements with herb gardens. From a coffee cup to an old PVC pipe or a wooden tub, there are different things you can use to grow herbs. You don't need a massive investment for gardening. Your windowsills, balcony, terrace, fire escape, and any other random containers can be fashioned into growing containers for herbs. Herbs are a great way to introduce green pockets into your living spaces. Brighten up the indoors and outdoors with an herb garden.

No Boring Meals

Adding a few fresh herbs can instantly elevate the flavor profile of any meals. A simple side dish can become the hero of a meal with fresh herbs such as basil, parsley, oregano, and so on. Go through the different list of herbs discussed in this book, and pick those that appeal to you. Once you start growing and tending the plants, you can harvest fresh herbs regularly.

Cost-Effective

Growing herbs and using them is cheaper than purchasing them from a grocery store. Herbs, especially the fresh ones, can be quite expensive when obtained from your local grocer. Usually, most varieties of fresh herbs are not easily available, and you need to go to specialty stores. This merely increases the costs involved. Purchasing seeds and growing them at home is quite simple and easy.

Educational

If you have any kids at home, growing herbs is a great educational tool. Whenever you grow a new plant, you can talk to your kids about it. It can become a family activity where everyone in the household tends to these plants regularly. Even if there are no kids at home, it will be an educational activity for you. When you start growing these herbs, you realize the different properties and benefits they offer. It also teaches you more about the environment and makes you conscious of where your food comes from.

Health Benefits

Gardening is a great stress buster. From sowing seeds to watching them germinate and grow into plants and reaping the harvest, it's exciting. It is also quite calming. If you're looking for a new hobby or a stress buster, try gardening herbs.

Chapter Two:

Garden Ideas

A great thing about herbs is you can grow them indoors and outdoors. Even if you have any space constraints, you can successfully create your herb garden with materials you can easily find. Yes, you don't need any expensive equipment or make a huge investment to create an herb garden. All it takes is a little creativity and wise use of space. Home gardening is a fun and quick way to ensure a supply of fresh herbs. You don't need any costly equipment to create your herb garden. All it takes is a little creativity. You can start your herb garden using coffee mugs or even PVC pipes. Here are some simple herb garden ideas to inspire you.

Tiered Hanging Basket

An old-fashioned hanging basket often used to place fruits on display can be easily converted into a hanging herb garden. You can hang it on the porch, balcony, or even a windowsill.

Wooden Box

Find an old wooden box and use it as a plant. Fill it with soil mixture and get planting. It's ideal for growing bushy herbs such as mint or basil. You can also decorate the wooden crate and create a table-top herb garden. Grow a couple of varieties of herbs to fill up the box.

Wagon Wheel

If you like the idea of a rustic herb garden, use an old wagon wheel. The spokes of a wagon wheel naturally help separate the herbs and add a rustic charm to the garden. This is more of an outdoor idea, and you can place it in your yard.

CD Tower

If you have an old CD tower, you can use it as a tiered stand for growing herbs. Place a few planters or containers with herbs and get started. You can get as creative as you want when it comes to decorating the CD tower.

Paint Cans

If you have any old paint cans lying in the house or dried up paint cans, fashion them into growing containers. Clean them thoroughly and paint the old paint cans. You can add some decals to show the name of the plant and get started. These stylish containers are ideal for growing herbs because they offer plenty of space for the roots to grow. You can use them as decorative items to spruce up any living spaces.

Herb Wheel

You need a hexagonal planter, which is split into six sections, to separate the herbs. Depending on your needs, this design can be easily expanded.

Coffee Or Teacups

Do you have any old coffee or teacups at home you no longer use? Instead of throwing them away, repurpose them into growing containers. Make things more creative, place them in a wicker basket, and start growing your favorite herbs.

Rain Gutters

Yes, you read it right, a rain gutter is a brilliant way to grow herbs. Their shallow design makes them perfect for simple herbs. Visit a local hardware store and purchase a rain gutter to start your indoor garden. Fixe the gutter on a wall and use it as a regular planter. Now, let your creativity guide the way. Paint the gutter, add decals to it, and decorate it any way you want. You can leave it the way it is to add some rustic charm to your home.

Bookshelf Garden

We all use bookshelves to store books and in pretty much anything we can think of. It is a versatile piece of furniture, and you can use it for more than just books. Create an indoor garden with an old bookshelf. To make things more interesting, place a couple of potted herbs and all the other books, magazines, and anything else you have on display.

One-Pot Garden

Perhaps the most straightforward idea to create an indoor garden is a big pot. Yes, all you need is a big pot. Select the different herbs you wish to grow, sow the seeds, and wait for them to sprout. The containers can also be divided to accommodate different herbs. If you don't want to do this, here is another simple idea for you. If you have any old corks at home, write the herb's name on the cork and spear it with an old fork or a skewer and place it in the pot with the herbs. It makes identifying the herbs quite easy and creates an aesthetic appeal.

Vertical Box Planter

If you like DIY projects, this is ideal for you. Vertical planters are easily available in the market, and if not, make one at home. It's essentially a large wooden box with multiple racks to accommodate the planters. A small vertical box planter can also be hanged from a wall to save floor space.

Hanging Planters

It's not just the floor space that can be used for gardening; even the ceiling space comes in handy. Small planters can be suspended from the ceiling. The planters come with a tray at the bottom to prevent water leakage.

Windowsill Garden

Using your windowsill is one of the most common techniques used in urban gardening. If the windowsill receives sufficient sunlight, you have found the right spot. Take a curtain rod and attach it so you can hang the herbs from the rod. Curtain hooks can be used for this purpose, and hanging planters will come in handy.

Pegboard

Find a pegboard or repurpose an old pegboard you have at home. All you need to do is grow herbs in small teacups or containers that can dangle from the pegboard. Place a pair of shears on the pegboard and harvest the herbs whenever you need them. Small pots and galvanized tales can also be used to accommodate herbs. This is an incredibly simple idea to execute and hardly takes up any space. It is also a great way to decorate a boring wall.

Mason Jars

Mason jars are not only attractive but are quite cheap to purchase. If you don't want to buy any mason jars, think about using old ones at home. You don't even need to paint the mason jars to spruce it up. Place them with the planted herbs on your kitchen countertop order a bookshelf in the living room. They can be placed on any flat surface of your choice. Instantly brighten a living space with herbs planted in a mason jar.

Upside Down Planters

Instead of regular planters, there are upside-down planters available these days that are ideal for high ceilings. Watering them is easy, and you can reach out and pluck herbs whenever you need it. You can either order them online or purchase them from exclusive gardening stores.

Apart from the ideas discussed in this section, there are other ideas you can use. Wooden tubs, wheelbarrows, wine racks, old buckets, and even wicker baskets can be used as planters. As mentioned earlier, all you need is a little creativity to start your herb garden.

Chapter Three:

Getting Started

After going through the benefits of growing herbs at home and different gardening ideas, you might be excited to get started. Before you do, it is important to learn about the steps involved in herb gardening.

Growing From Seeds or Cuttings

As mentioned, herbs require a lot of sunlight. Start the seeds at least 6-8 weeks before the last frost date. It gives them sufficient time to germinate and thrive when the sun is out and warm. Never plant the seeds too deeply or shallowly because it results in poor germination. A simple rule of thumb you can remember while sowing seeds is to place them about 2-3 times as deep as the container's diameter. Most tiny seeds, such as coriander, mustard, or fenugreek, do well when sown closer to the surface. Allow the sunlight to germinate them, and the plastic around top ensures they don't dry up. After sowing the seeds, gently press into them such that the soil surface is visible, but don't push them deep into the container. The seeds need to have sufficient contact with the soil, which prompts them to germinate when the soil reaches the right temperature. Certain herbs such as cilantro, poppies, and parsley require lower soil temperature than ones ideal for hot weather, such as basil.

Some herbs grow well from seeds, while others do better with cuttings. If you decide to grow from seeds, purchase good-quality seeds from a local nursery, gardening store, or order them online. Plant the seeds for the concerned herb in a separate pot or container, pack it loosely with soil and nutrient mixture, and water them regularly. To encourage germination and easy drainage, place the pots in a sunny spot. Before you do this, cover the pots or containers with a plastic bag or cling film to retain their moisture.

The ideal temperature for germination is between 60-73°F. Make a point to check the pots regularly to ensure the soil is still moist and lightly mist it with water as required. Remove the plastic wrapping or bag from the pot or container as soon as the seedlings appear. Ensure that you place the pots in a warm and sunny location for a couple of hours daily, and water them regularly.

The next option you can consider while starting an herb garden is growing from cuttings. This is an equally rewarding procedure. The first thing you need is to select a stem from a mature plant and use it as a cutting. Perhaps the easiest option available is to grow herbs from cuttings of softwood stems. The ideal time to do this is to take the cutting from the plant during spring or early summer and transplant it to grow in another container. What is a softwood cutting? It's the pliable green stems towards the lower part of the plant section. Semi-hardwood cuttings are slightly brown, and they are ideal for growing in soil and sand instead of water. In comparison, softwood cuttings can easily grow in water.

Select a plant you wish to take the cuttings from and take several of them. Ideally, the cuttings need to be at least 20 cm in length. The cuttings should be obtained from the plant right below the leaf node without any leaves towards the top leaf nodes above the cut you made. Once you have the cuttings in place, place them in the desired water container with the soil mixture. Once again, it's time to cover the container and the cutting with a plastic bag or cling film. Anywhere between 3-4 weeks, the cuttings will take root, and you can see small leaves appear.

Steps to Follow

Neither a front nor backyard is required to start an herb garden. You also don't need to spend hours together, maintaining this garden. Irrespective of how busy your life gets, herb gardening is simple. In this section, let's look at the different things you need to consider before you start gardening.

Soil

Herbs are quite sturdy, and often grow wherever you let them. Loamy soil with a combination of silt, sand, and organic matter is well suited for herbs. They thrive in well-drained soil. Soil also contains a mixture of organic matter, different helpful microorganisms, and minerals. Since the soil is the natural source of nutrients, clay or loamy soil is ideal for herbs. The organic matter, sand, and silt in it should contain sufficient nitrogen, potassium, and phosphorus for the herbs to grow. The ideal range of pH for growing herbs should be between 6-7.5.

Light

Before you gather any supplies, find the right spot for the herb garden. Irrespective of whether it's your patio, kitchen windowsill, or the terrace, plant them in an area with sufficient sunlight. They don't need to be directly exposed to sunlight and need shade, so they don't burn. If you are growing them indoors, place them in sunlight every day for a few hours (at least 4). You can also consider using grow lights if you do want to grow them outdoors.

Fertilizer

Herbs need different nutrients for their growth, such as potassium, nitrogen, phosphorus, Sulphur, magnesium, copper, sodium, nickel, boron, chlorine, iron, zinc, and manganese. Most of these nutrients are naturally found in soil, and replenishing it from time to time ensures the plants get all the nutrients they need. For instance, nitrogen keeps the leaves, green, and promotes their growth.

While phosphorus is important for the roots and potassium activates essential enzymatic reactions. There are organic and inorganic fertilizers easily available these days. The ideal ratio of nitrogen, phosphorus, and potassium for fertilizers is 5:10:10. It essentially means a 10-pound bag of fertilizer contains half-pound nitrogen and 1 pound each of potassium and phosphorus. These fertilizers can be obtained in granular and liquid form. The granular fertilizers are a source of dry nutrients and need to be incorporated with the soil. Liquid fertilizers merely need to be diluted with water and sprinkle on the soil.

Compost

Herbs thrive when they get sufficient sunlight without direct exposure and are grown in well-drained soil. Heavy clay soil is ideal for growing herbs, and adding a little extra compost ensures your plants get all the organic matter they need. Store-bought compost is a mix of rotted organic matter and other simple ingredients such as coconut fiber and peat. Always opt for high-quality compost. You can add a little perlite or vermiculture to the soil to enhance its drainage. Water retention tends to spoil the roots of the herbs and, therefore, don't overwater the plants.

Seeds or Cuttings

Depending on the kind of containers you want use and the sunlight available, you need to decide what herbs you wish to grow. The simplest way to create your garden is by purchasing potted plants or herbs and tending to them. However, if you truly want to derive the pleasures of gardening, start with seeds. Some plant varieties are better to start with seeds.

In the previous section, you were given information about growing herbs from seeds and cuttings. Once you find a good spot to grow the herbs, have the necessary soil and containers, it's time to decide whether you want to grow from seeds or cuttings. If you are just getting started with gardening, and want to see quick results, cuttings will help. However, growing herbs from seeds are quite simple too. All it takes is a little extra time and patience. With the right tools and a little patient, growing herbs is incredibly simple.

Garden Ideas

From indoor gardens to vertical gardening and growing in small containers, there are different options available. You no longer have to worry about the availability of growing space. The great thing about herbs is they are versatile and can be easily grown in any type of garden you opt for. Space is no longer a constraint with urban gardening, and you don't have to limit yourself. You will learn more about this in the next chapter.

Pests

Common pests that tend to trouble plants in any type of garden are slugs, fungus, aphids, and whiteflies. Blight and powdery mildew are other common types of fungus you need to watch out for. If you notice a powdery white layer or grey fuzz on plants, it's blight! The simplest way to deal with any form of pest is to prune and stake plants for better air continuous circulation. You can use insecticides, pesticides, and fungicides to treat all this. Since you will be continuously harvesting herbs, the chances of all this are quite less. Using crushed eggshells and some gravel around the base of the plant prevents insects from crawling and feasting on your beloved herbs.

Once you start growing, all you need to do is harvest and replant if required. The great thing about herbs is even if you don't use them immediately, you can dry and store them after harvesting. Leave them out to dry in natural sunlight or dehydrate them using an oven or a microwave. Once they are fully dried, store them in airtight containers, and they will last you for at least any.

Chapter Four:

Top 10 Best Herbs to Grow

Growing herbs isn't rocket science. Herbs are generally more forgiving than flowering and other fruit-bearing varieties. In this section, let's look at the herbs best suited for a beginner's herb garden.

Basil

One of the best herbs you can grow is basil. The luscious green and aromatic leaves of basil truly make it wonderful. There are several basil versions, such as the sweet basil, Italian basil, Thai basil, and even purple basil. The most common variety is the sweet basil with slightly round and dark green leaves. This bushy herb can grow up to two feet in height. Basil not only adds flavor to soups, stews, sauces, and salads but offers a variety of health benefits too. Freshly brewed basil tea helps fights indigestion, soothe headaches, stop cough, and even reduce stress.

How to Grow Basil

Basil needs plenty of sunlight to grow and thrive. If you are growing them indoors, ensure the plants get at least 6-8 hours of sunlight daily. Just because they love sunlight, doesn't mean you leave them out in the sun every day. If the leaves welt or have a yellow tinge, it means they are getting too much sun. The simplest way to let them recover is by placing them in a shady location.

Depending on the climatic conditions, the amount of water basil requires differs. As a rule of thumb, never let the soil dry out while growing basil. A simple way to test it is to place your finger in the soil, and if it is dry, water the plant. You can use the same technique, even for herbs that are growing outdoors. Always use tepid water, and ensure the pot has sufficient holes for drainage. If there are any small leaves present near the base of the stem, remove them because they prevent water from reaching the roots. Never let the plant retain any excess water, or it can result in fungal attacks.

The ideal type of soil for growing basil outdoors is a loamy variety. If you are growing indoors, consider using a soilless mixture that consists of peat and aged bark in equal proportions. You can also use a mixture that contains perlite, wood chips, and sphagnum in equal proportions.

The ideal temperature for basil is around 70°F. It is not ideal for cold climatic conditions and will die when exposed to extremely cold weather. If you want to use fertilizer, ensure that it contains nitrogen, potassium, and phosphorus, in the ratio of 10:10:10.

It would be best if you pruned the basil plants to ensure their optimal health regularly. If the herbs are kept indoors, try to repot the plant when you decide to prune. Start cutting the leaves right above the second visible grouping of leaves. Leave the leaves close to the soil the way they are to promote better growth. After this, you can prune the leaves, so the plant is about 1/3rd its size. It essentially means you need to prune basil plants once every 3-4 weeks for a good harvest.

Sweet basil is an annual plant. The flowers might look pretty, but it is not desirable to let the basil plants bloom because it marks their life cycle. As soon as the buds appear, nip them. Also, the leaves' taste is altered after a flowering cycle, and the leaves can taste pungent and slightly bitter.

Gently pluck the leaves whenever you need and avoid any jerky movements. If you are rough while plucking the leaves, it can shock the plant's system, especially the roots. Whenever you pluck the leaves, pluck close to the stem and use shears. If you notice any dried, yellow, or wilted leaves, prune them immediately.

Japanese beetle, slugs, and snails are the common pests and insects you need to watch out for. You will learn more about dealing with common pests and insects towards the end of this chapter.

Chives

As with basil, there are different varieties of chives available. The most common varieties are the Chinese or garlic chives and onion chives. This herb belongs to the lily family and has a flavorful and slightly pungent aroma making it ideal for salads, dressings, and other forms of cooking. The chive plant has a small bulb, much like an onion plant, and it stays underground while its stalks are harvested. The herb can grow to up to 20 inches in length and about 1/2-inch in diameter. When in full bloom, chives have purple star-shaped tiny flowers.

Not just cooking, but there are several other ways in which you can use chives. There are believed to be natural pet represents and can be used to deter pests and insects from attacking other herbs. The most common pests chives repel are aphids and mildew. Boil some chives with water, and once the water cools down, you can spray this mixture around other herbs and protect them from mildew. Chives are believed to have antibacterial, anti-viral, and anti-inflammatory properties. So, start adding chives to your cooking to improve your overall health and tackle inflammation.

How to Grow Chives

Growing chives is quite simple, and they are ideal for indoor and outdoor herb gardens. Chives generally like the sun and require a lot of daily sunlight. However, if you live in regions with high temperatures, ensure the chives get some shade during noon, or the stalks can burn. The spot you choose for chives should get sufficient sunlight of at least 8 hours daily. Ideally, the less powerful and slightly warm rays of the morning sun will do, instead of harsh sunlight. If your chives get too much or too little sun, they will not grow like supposed to.

There are no hard and fast rules about watering chives. Ensure the top inch of the soil never stays dry, and if it is dry, water the plant regularly. As with basil, you need to mist the chive plants, especially if the surroundings aren't humid. After you mist or water, these plants ensure the water drains out properly. If the water doesn't rain out, it causes root rot, and the chive bulbs will not survive. While watering the chives, ensure that the soil is completely soaked with tepid water, and it drains out thoroughly. The containers or the pots you are growing the chives in should have sufficient drainage holes. As the plant starts growing, you can reduce the frequency of watering.

The ideal combination of soil to grow chives is a mixture of sand or loamy soil with organic compost. If the soil doesn't drain easily and retains moisture, it spoils the health of the plant. There isn't any specific temperature range for chives, but a colder climate slows down their growth rate. The ideal mixture of nitrogen, potassium, and phosphorus in fertilizer for chives is 20:20:20. If there is more nitrogen than this, the plants will not survive. Granule or liquid fertilizers work well for these plants.

Harvesting chives is quite simple. You merely need to cut the plant stems while leaving 2 inches above the soil. Start with the outside leaves and slowly make your way inward. Wait until the plant is about 6 inches tall, and then you can harvest it. Chives tend to flower periodically, and the flowers look quite pretty. Unlike basil, you don't have to worry about flowering in this plant cycle. Once the flower blooms and dies, the stem starts growing right back.

You cannot dry chives and use them because it spoils their entire flavor and texture fresh chives are the best way to go. If you want to preserve or store chives, freezing is a good option. Harvest the chives and place them in an airtight container and store it in the freezer. Alternatively, you can fill up water in ice trays and add some chives to it.

Dill

Dill is believed to be native to the Mediterranean region. Several European cultures used dill in cooking and for healing purposes too. Records date dill's medicinal usage back to 3000 years. Dill is believed to stimulate courage and bravery, and for the same reasons, gladiators were fed dill in ancient Rome. It is an annual herb and can grow up to 24 inches tall. Dill has a thin stem with small pine-like soft leaves that are anywhere between 4-8 inches in length. It isn't a flowering variety, but it does produce white and yellow blossoms. This is commonly added to pickles, stews, casseroles, soups, pasta, and meat and fish dishes to enhance their flavor. It's widely used in French cooking.

Apart from cooking, dill also has medicinal values. It's a common home remedy to treat colic in babies and is a sleep remedy. A brew made of hot milk and dill leaves is an ancient Indian remedy believed to promote better sleep. It can soothe stomach problems, such as indigestion and diarrhea. It is also used as a breath freshener.

How to Grow Dill

Don't be fooled by its delicate appearance because dill is a sturdy herb. It's a hot weather plant and requires a lot of sunlight. It doesn't bloom frequently, but if it starts flowering, the leaf production stops. Morning sun, afternoon shade, and keeping away from the harshest sun, ensure the dill leaves grow well. It can be grown indoors and outdoors. If you are growing it indoors, ensure it gets at least 6-8 hours of natural sunlight daily. If not natural sunlight, artificial growing lights such as fluorescent lights are a good idea.

Its delicate structure means the plant stands the risk of being overwatered. Ideally, it would be best to dig small furrows in the soil and slowly water this plant. Ensure the water never falls directly on the stem, or it can spoil the herb. The long roots of this plant ensure they ideally seek out water, even from depths. Insert your index finger into the soil around the plant and check if it is overwatered. If it seems fairly dry, slowly water the roots. Once again, it's important to ensure there's sufficient drainage in the growing container.

Any light and medium-textured soil is a good choice for growing dill. As long as it provides good drainage, you don't have to worry about it. Adding a little organic compost certainly enhances its overall growth. The ideal temperatures to grow dill is between 43-79°F. If the weather is too cold, the frost will kill the dill leaves. You don't need any specific fertilizer to grow dill. A little organic compost made of kitchen scraps is more than enough. You don't even need to add any fertilizer, and the herb will grow on its own.

Pruning the herb is quite important when it comes to dill, especially if there are flowers. Pluck the buds away to stimulate leaf production. The ideal time to harvest dill is early in the morning because its flavor content is rather high. You don't need to buy more dill seeds, and instead, wait for some plants to flower and then harvest the seeds to grow more.

Harvesting and storing dill plants is quite simple- pluck the leaves whenever you need but allow at least 2 inches of the stem after you harvest the herb, dry, and preserve it in an airtight container. You can also freeze these leaves for later.

Oregano

This herb is native to the Mediterranean region and belongs to the organum family. The herb can be anywhere between 8-32 inches tall, and its leaves can be up to 1.5 inches long. Its strong and spicy flavor makes it an ideal culinary herb. It is commonly used in French and Italian cooking. The small purple flowers produced by the oregano plant are quite pretty to look at. Pasta or pizza sauce without oregano is impossible to even think of. Apart from this, it can be used to make dyes and is a traditional remedy to treat stomach cramps, tonsillitis, and headaches. Oregano oils can be used in soaps and to treat athletes' foot. A brew made with fresh or dried oregano leaves is an ancient medicinal remedy popular in Crete.

How to Grow Oregano

Growing oregano is fairly simple, but as with any other herbs, there are certain considerations you need to consider Irrespective of whether it's an indoor or outdoor plant, ensure it gets sunlight for at least half the day. Sunlight improves the aroma of oregano leaves and encourages the plant to grow. However, you cannot grow them in extremely hot conditions because they can quickly scorch the leaves. Place the oregano plants near a window that receives a lot of sunlight. You cannot overwater these plants as long as they have sufficient drainage.

Most oregano plants are drought resistant and don't need to be watered excessively.

Similarly, they don't like extremely humid conditions, either. They thrive in areas with low humidity. Water these plants only when the topsoil is dry to touch.

Oregano often grows in rocky terrain, which offers good drainage. It also has long roots that actively seek water from the soil. Loamy soil, coupled with some gravel, helps stimulate its natural soil requirement. A mixture of potting soil, peat moss, and perlite in equal ratio also works well. The ideal temperature to grow oregano is between 55-70°F for both indoor and outdoor varieties.

Organic fertilizers such as fishmeal, worm castings, and bone meal are brilliant for oregano. Even if you purchase any chemical fertilizer, ensure the ratio of nitrogen, phosphorus, and potassium, and it is 10:10:10. Be wary of any fertilizers that include an excess of nitrogen, because it reduces the flavor of the leaves.

You need to frequently prune the oregano herb to enhance the air circulation around the plant and reduce its risk of diseases. If the leaves start bunching together, it means you need to prune the area. Start pruning the leaves once the plant is about 3 inches tall. The ideal time to harvest oregano is right before it starts blooming. If you like oregano leaves with a strong, pungent aroma, then nip the leaves as soon as the flowers start showing up. A great thing about oregano is it can be harvested throughout the season.

Oregano leaves taste good in fresh and dried forms. You can dry them in an oven at around 200°F or leave them out in the sun. Once they are dry, simply place them in an airtight container and store them. Alternatively, you can also infuse them with olive oil and use it for cooking.

Marjoram

Marjoram is an herb indigenous to regions of Cyprus and Turkey. It's a perineal herb with oval and elongated leaves. The leaves can be approximately 0.2-0.5 inches in length and have woody stems. When in bloom, it has small white or lilac-colored flowers. Marjoram shares certain similarities with oregano. The only difference is its distinct hints of pine and citrus. Its citrusy taste makes it a great addition to gravies, salads, sauces, and any other dishes using meats. Apart from cooking, it's believed to be rich in antioxidants. Tea steeped with Marjoram helps relieve nausea, tackle indigestion, reduce stomach cramps, fight diarrhea, constipation, and even relieve mild headaches.

How to Grow Marjoram

Growing Marjoram isn't difficult, because it is a sturdy herb and can withstand severe weather conditions. It grows well when exposed to sunlight daily, but it doesn't need harsh lights. While growing indoors, ensure it gets sufficient natural light. Water this plant only when there are any signs of dryness of the soil. Marjoram isn't drought resistant like oregano, and therefore, you need to water it daily. Loamy soil is the ideal choice for growing Marjoram, or any other type of well-draining soil will do. The ideal temperature for Marjoram is between 62-76°F.

The quality of soil is the only thing you need to consider when it comes to growing Marjoram. If the soil isn't loamy, mixing it with a little organic matter helps. Ideally, fertilize the soil before you sow the seeds, and it enhances their overall growth rate. Unless you prune the marjoram plant regularly, it doesn't produce new leaves. All the older branches need to be removed that don't produce leaves. Try to harvest it before the flowers appear, or else the taste becomes slightly better. Plucking the buds helps ensure better foliage.

You can use it the way you use oregano, and the same techniques can be used for preservation too. Freezing it, storing it in olive oil, or merely drying and placing it in an airtight container helps.

Mint

Mint is commonly used in various countries across the globe and isn't restricted to a specific region. It is a perineal plant and has plants like stamps. It has oblong leaves with serrated edges that often grow in opposite pairs on each stem. There are different varieties of mint, and it is an invasive variety. Depending on the type of mint you decide to grow, its leaves can range from dark green to purple hues. The plant can grow up to 45 inches in height. Mint has a refreshing aroma that can easily liven up any meal you wish to cook. It pairs well with red meats and can be used in salads, sauces, ice creams, and stews. Spearmint and peppermint are believed to be natural pest repellents and help keep ants and aphids away from other plants. A tea brewed with fresh mint leaves can relieve headaches and has a calming effect. A fresh cup of mint tea can also help soothe an upset stomach.

How to Grow Mint

Mint grows quite easily, and if you are not careful, it can soon overwhelm your entire garden. Grow mint in a separate pot or a container to contain its growth. It can be easily grown indoors and outdoors. If you are growing it indoors, ensure that it gets sufficient sunlight daily. Mint thrives when exposed to sunlight and need up to 8 hours of daily sunlight. However, keep it away from the harsh sun because it can scorch the leaves. Overwatering mint can quickly destroy the plant. The leaves turn brown or black when overwatered. Therefore, ensure that sufficient drainage is available in the container before you start watering if the top layer of the soil is dry to touch, water the plant. Soil quality and humidity are important when it comes to mint. Sandy soil that doesn't hold extra water offers excellent drainage. Poor quality soil holds onto more water than required and, therefore, mixing a little perlite, and peat increases water drainage. The ideal temperature to Grow mint is between 54- 85 °F. In higher temperatures, the growth of the plant tends to slow down. The ideal ratio of fertilizer firm Mint is nitrogen, phosphorus, and potassium, in the ratio of 10:10:10.

You need to constantly harvest and prune mint if you want it to grow. Do not forget to cut the stems and branches to prevent overcrowding. Ideally, harvest it before it starts flowering. Whenever you cut mint leaves, ensure that you start after leaving at least 2 inches of the stem from the soil. You can also pick the leaves and cut the stems as and when required. Storing and preserving mint is quite easy. You can freeze them, dry and store them, or pluck fresh leaves depending on your convenience.

Parsley

Parsley is quite popular in the Mediterranean region and is believed to be native to this region. The most commonly used form of parsley in cooking is flat-leaf parsley. It is an annual plant with bright green colored foliage. The leaves often come together to form rosettes and can grow up to 4 inches in diameter. The plant can grow up to 36 inches in length, and it is relatively simple to grow. Parsley can be easily added to stews, casseroles, sauces, and also as a garnish. You can also infuse olive oil with parsley and use it for cooking. There are several medicinal uses of parsley, too. Parsley juice can ease bladder infections, reduce blood pressure, and fight eye infections. Ingesting parsley in the form of teas is the easiest way to consume it. Rubbing crushed parsley leaves on any insect bites helps reduce any itchy sensation.

How to Grow Parsley

As with any other herb, there are certain environmental factors you need to consider to grow parsley at home. They usually grow into lush bushes, which will brighten up any living space. They need anywhere between 4-8 hours of daily sunlight. If natural sunlight isn't available, ensure that it gets sufficient artificial growing lights. The long roots of parsley plants can tap into deeper layers of soil in search of water. Generally, you don't need to water these plants daily, and even watering them once a week helps. All this depends on the external weather conditions. If the weather is too hot, you need to water the plants frequently. If it is too humid, reduce the water frequency.

Once again, check the top layer of the soil to determine whether the roots need more water. Loamy soil is the best choice to grow parsley. You can also consider adding mulch to the soil to increase its growth. The ideal combination of mulch should include dried pine bark. The desired temperature to grow parsley is between 50-75°F. If the temperature increases or reduces below these levels, it slows down the growth of parsley. The composition of fertilizer ideal for growing parsley is 5:10:5 for nitrogen: phosphorus: potassium.

Start pruning the parsley leaves as soon as the plant is about 8 inches tall. Pluck the leaves in a bunch and use it for cooking. Don't forget to prune the stems, especially the dried and weak ones. The outer leaves tend to mature quickly. If there are any yellow or wilted leaves, remove them immediately. Try to cut the stems about an inch close to the soil to promote better growth.

Dry the parsley after harvest and store it in an airtight container. Alternatively, you can also freeze the fresh leaves in ice cube trays with water.

Rosemary

Rosemary is native to the Mediterranean region-Greece, North Africa, Italy, Spain, southern France, and Portugal. It grows well in humid, sunny, and rocky terrain. This culinary herb has certain medicinal properties too. It is believed to be introduced to Britain by the Romans during the 8th century. This herb can grow up to 25-70 inches long and has spiky green leaves. When in bloom, it produces tiny bluish flowers.

Rosemary pairs brilliantly well with red meats, chicken, vegetables and can also be infused with desserts for a savory tinge. You can add it to sauces, stews, and curries. Alternatively, olive oil infused with rosemary makes for an excellent cooking medium. Rosemary oil is believed to have natural pain-relieving properties and can also help with external healing. Rubbing rosemary essential oil diluted with any carrier oil on bruised regions promotes healing. Rosemary's natural aroma makes it an ideal addition to room fresheners too.

How to Grow Rosemary

It is a hardy herb and can sustain harsh conditions. However, there are some growing factors you must consider. While growing indoors, place it next to a large window that receives natural light or under a skylight. Since it thrives in the Mediterranean region, this herb loves the sunny and humid outdoors. Once the plant reaches maturity, its watering needs decrease. As long as the top layer of soil is moist to touch, you don't have to water it. Since it grows in rocky terrain, ensure there is plenty of drainage in the pot, and there is no excess water. Well-draining sandy soil mixed with gravel works brilliantly well for growing rosemary. Ideally, the external weather should not be lower than 30°F for rosemary to grow and thrive. It can tolerate hot temperatures but ensure it isn't directly exposed to harsh sunlight throughout the day. If you live in cold regions, ensure that you move the rosemary plants to warm spots. Using slow-release fertilizer works especially well to promote the growth of young plants. Any store-bought fertilizer or organic compost can be used.

If you notice any yellowing leaves or broken stems, prune the plant immediately. The ideal time to harvest rosemary is just before the flowers start appearing. Wait for at least a year before you start harvesting rosemary. If you ever need a few leaves, you can snip them off the plant now and then. However, don't harvest it fully when it is in full bloom. After harvesting, you can easily dry this herb under the sunlight or even in an oven. Freezing rosemary doesn't work because they often go black. If you want to freeze them, ensure that you thoroughly coat the rosemary leaves with olive oil and freeze them.

Sage

Did you know that most of the Sage available in the market these days comes from the regions of Montenegro, Croatia, and Albania? It is native to the Mediterranean region, especially the northern coast. Sage is also one of the most important exports of Yugoslavia. It's a brilliant culinary herb with various medicinal uses. The history of Sage goes back to 16th century Europe, where it was commonly used for cooking. However, it was used even before this by the Romans for medicinal purposes. It can grow up to 30 inches tall and has long and narrow leaves. Sage is believed to have healing properties and produces pretty flowers, which are often pink, purple, and white. There are different varieties of Sage available. Sage is commonly used in savory dishes, and it pairs extremely well with all types of meats. Sage is rich in antioxidants and has anti-inflammatory properties. Fresh tea steeped with Sage can reduce sore throat, night sweats caused due to menopause, and excessive sweating. When you burn dried sage it acts as a natural pest repellant.

How to Grow Sage

Sage is a resilient variety, and growing it at home is easy. With this herb, you don't have to worry about excessive sunlight because they need at least 6-8 hours of sunlight daily. Don't forget to place them in a spot with plenty of natural light or provide them with sufficient artificial growing lights. If you leave them in the shade for long periods, it stunts its growth. Ensure you water these plants fairly regularly and don't leave them unwatered for prolonged periods. Likewise, if you overwater it, it will rot their roots and kill the plant immediately. Loamy soil works extremely well for this herb. The ideal growing temperature is between 60-80°F. If the temperature is less than 40°F, Sage will not grow. Any standard fertilizer works fairly well with these plants, and they don't need specific fertilizers. However, don't start overfeeding the plants.

The general lifespan of a sage plant is between 4-5 years, and after this, they tend to become woodier and lose their natural flavor. Therefore, try to prune this herb as much as you possibly can to increase its foliage. Generally, Sage is pruned once it starts flowering. Try to cut it down to half its size, starting with the woody stems. Don't prune the lower levels of the leaves because it can harm the health of the plant. You can harvest the leaves whenever required. If you want to harvest in large batches, ensure you do it right before the flowers start appearing. Even dried sage leaves taste as good as the fresh varieties. Place them on a wax paper and let them dry naturally. Once they are dried, crunch them and see them in an airtight container. As with other herbs, you can also freeze it.

Thyme

Thyme is also native to the Mediterranean region. However, various ancient cultures in Egypt and Greece used it for embalming and some religious purposes. Ancient Romans also used it to flavor their food, cheese, and beverages. It looks like a small shrub with bright pink or lavender flowers and the most common varieties of thyme are English thyme, lemon thyme, and caraway thyme. Any Mediterranean styled dish can do with a little thyme in it. It is often found in several commercially produced hand sanitizers and mouthwashes. A tea brewed with thyme leaves can reduce blood pressure and reduce coughing. It can also enhance your overall immunity. Thyme is commonly used in disinfectants and, when rubbed on the skin, acts as a mosquito repellant.

How to Grow Thyme

As long as thyme gets 6 hours of natural sunlight daily, it will thrive. Avoid placing them in shady areas as it can stunt the growth. Ensure that you water the plant daily to prevent the soil from drying up. Any type of loamy soil or soil with good drainage is an ideal choice. Temperature isn't much of an issue as long as the weather doesn't get extremely hot or cold.

Deal With Pests and Insects

Herbs contain certain aromatic compounds that act as a natural insect and pest repellants. Certain herbs can also repel pests from other plants around them. However, as a gardener, it is your responsibility to take care of all the plants you grow, and herbs are not an exception. If you want to protect or rescue your herbs, ensure you treat the plant at the right stage. The most common pests you need to watch out for our Japanese beetle, leaf miners, slugs and snails, spider mites, aphids, and scale. These pests can turn the leaves yellow, attack its roots, eat the foliage, suck out the sap, or result in pinprick spots and pucker the leaves.

So, how can you protect your herbs from these pests? The simplest way to do this is by ensuring the plants are always in good health, have sufficient wiggle room, and are thoroughly watered. If you notice any infested areas, remove them immediately and throw them before the problem starts to spread. If there are any small infestations, dislodge them with a hose if the plant is strong enough. If there are any larger insects, you can handpick and throw them away. A non-toxic insecticidal soap mixed with water and sprayed on the herbs can also be helpful. Lacewings and ladybugs can be used to repel other pests and insects. A simple tip you need to keep in mind before using herbs- even if they are organically grown, thoroughly rinse them with water.

Chapter Five:

Common Mistakes to Avoid While Growing Herbs

Herb gardening is quite simple, and there are different ideas you can use to start your herb garden. Irrespective of whether you have a huge backyard or live in an apartment, herb gardening isn't space specific. Getting started with an herb garden is certainly exciting. To increase your chances of success, here are some common mistakes you should avoid.

Not Nourishing The Soil

Paying attention to the soil you use is one of the first things you should do before growing herbs. If you don't use fresh garden or potting soil, the plants will not grow. Also, don't forget to continuously replenish the soil to replace all the nutrients the plant absorbs while growing. Simple ways to replenish soil include adding coffee grounds and crushed eggshells to the containers. These organic soil amendments help balance the pH levels and add extra nutrients. You can also make compost with kitchen scraps and leftovers. You have the option of using commercial fertilizers to enhance the nutrient composition of the soil. While using any commercial fertilizers, carefully go through the instructions on the package and dilutes them accordingly.

Not Providing The Plants Sufficient Light

Plants need sufficient sunlight to grow. If natural light isn't available, you need to use artificial grow lights. Ideally, when it comes to an herb garden, opt for south-facing windows or a sun porch to ensure they get sufficient sunlight. Most herbs require at least 4-6 hours of daily sunlight. If this cannot be obtained naturally, there are different artificial grow lights available. Most plants are often happy with fluorescent lightings, such as T8 or T12 standard tubes, high output T5 tubes, fluorescent light bulbs, and compact fluorescent lamps. To mimic the natural quality of light, opt for full-spectrum lights. As the number of plants you grow increases, the light bulbs should also increase.

Not Pruning

If you want your herbs to grow properly, you need to prune them regularly. For instance, basil needs to be pruned regularly to ensure it grows into a sturdy bush. Never prune the bottom leaves because there are important for the plant's health. Ensure the first cut you make is always at least 2-3 inches above the soil and doesn't include the growing set of leaves. Trim closely along the growing set of leaves to increase the plant's growth. If you don't follow these steps with pruning, you'll end up with a tall and spindly plant with hardly any leaves.

Not Watering The Plants Correctly

Watering the plants is important, and herbs are not an exception. Usually, most houseplants are watered deeply once a week. Well, you need to change this rule if you're used to it. Herbs need to be watered daily and only need a little water. Watering regularly ensures the plants get sufficient water to grow. The soil used should be light and airy, so the roots don't start decomposing. Instead of watering them with water can, you can mist them with a spray can.

Not Keeping Things Simple

Since you're just getting started with an herb garden, it's quintessential to keep things simple. Making things difficult at this stage and starting with any ambitious plants can quickly stifle your confidence and interest in gardening. Instead, start with easy a few easy to grow herbs and hardy variants such as basil. Go through the list of herbs discussed in this book, and their growing requirements to find one that interests you.

Not Learning About Different Herbs

Different herbs have different growing requirements, and you cannot use this same technique for every herb. Make it a point to learn more about different types of herbs available. Carefully go through the information given in this book about the ten best varieties of herbs and start with them. As you gain more confidence, learn more about different variations of these herbs. For instance, there are several varieties of mint, oregano, and basil.

Not Dealing With Pests

Always be prepared to deal with pests and other forms of invasive takeovers. You need to tend to the herbs regularly to prevent any weeds from growing. Likewise, pay attention to the pot or container in which the plants are grown.

Not Being Prepared

Once you start growing herbs, be prepared to be overwhelmed with a bounty of fresh herbs. Start sharing the herbs you grow with others and save some for later. You merely need to try out these herbs and store them in airtight containers or you can freeze the herbs, add them to oil or butter, or dry them. There are different ways in which you can use herbs and preserve them for up to one year.

Conclusion

By now, you would have realized how easy it is to start an herb garden. All it takes is some knowledge, care, time, and patience. You can create your little paradise with a little herb garden and enjoy fresh herbs whenever you want. There are a couple of things you must know before starting an herb garden, and all this information is provided within this book. Now, all that's left for you to do is select the herbs you like, the garden setting, which appeals to you and purchase the required seeds. Once all these things are in place, it's time to get started.

Now that you are equipped with the information you need to start an herb garden, the next step is to gather the supplies and get gardening.

Resources

Arnold, V. (2014, March 6). Herb Gardening for Beginners. Intoxicated On Life website: https://www.intoxicatedonlife.com/herb-gardening-beginners/

Brannan, A. (2017, June 16). Secrets to Herb Gardening for Beginners. Earth's Friends website: https://www.earthsfriends.com/herb-gardening-for-beginners/

Frowine, S. (n.d.). How to Deal with Pests in Herb Gardens. dummies website: https://www.dummies.com/home-garden/gardening/how-to-deal-with-pests-in-herb-gardens/

Herb Gardening for Beginners. (n.d.). www.tastefulgarden.com website: https://www.tastefulgarden.com/Herb-Gardening-for-Beginners-d19.htm

Shifler, A. (2019, May 29). Fertilizer for herbs: Benefits, types, and how to fertilize. Herbs at Home website: https://herbsathome.co/fertilizer-for-herbs/

Made in the USA
Monee, IL
20 September 2025

26167132R10036